BRANDING BRILLIANCE BLUEPRINT

Navigating your Visual Identity

Leela Tripathi

Crafting A Clear And Compelling Brand Narrative For Success

In our voyage through the realm of educational branding, we've unveiled the profound significance of consistency and resonance in sculpting your school's visual identity. As educators and administrators, you're architects of not just education, but of a legacy that echoes your institution's core values. Your journey towards brand excellence just received an exhilarating boost with the introduction of the "Blue Book of Branding"—an invaluable companion meticulously designed to elevate your branding journey.

Within the treasure trove of the "Blue Book," you'll discover a meticulously crafted step-by-step guide. This guide is your compass to navigate the uncharted waters of creating digital branding assets—be it logos, color schemes, typography, or visual content—that breathe life into your institution's essence. It's more than a guide; it's a roadmap that ensures every branding piece —whether it's a vibrant social media post, an elegant brochure, or a captivating website banner—resonates harmoniously with your institution's captivating narrative.

Unlocking the Power of the "Blue Book of Branding": Your Journey to Iconic Identity

By immersing yourself in the profound insights encapsulated within the pages of the "Blue Book of Branding," you're embarking on a transformative journey—one that empowers you to wield the extraordinary impact of a visually striking identity. Imagine this guide not merely as a manual, but as a magical tome that grants you the power to summon a brand identity that speaks volumes, leaving an indelible mark etched upon the very hearts of your stakeholders.

Crafting an Identity that Roars Volumes

Every stroke of your institution's visual representation communicates a message—a message that extends far beyond mere aesthetics. It's a language that resonates deep within the souls of those who encounter it. The "Blue Book of Branding" equips you with the tools to wield this language masterfully. By translating its teachings into captivating design elements, you'll forge a brand identity that roars volumes, capturing attention and imagination in equal measure.

Forging Connections that Transcend

As educators and administrators, your goal extends beyond imparting knowledge; it's about fostering profound connections. The "Blue Book of Branding" becomes your conduit to achieve this very objective. Through its guidance, you'll not only design visuals but also craft experiences—experiences that cut through the noise, resonate with authenticity, and transcend the ordinary. It's through these experiences that you'll forge connections that surpass transactional interactions, touching the realm of emotional resonance.

Amplifying Authenticity

In a world inundated with fleeting visuals, authenticity stands as the beacon that guides discerning eyes. The "Blue Book of Branding" empowers you to infuse this authenticity into every pixel, color, and curve. As you apply its principles, your branding will cease to be a mere representation—it will become a mirror reflecting your institution's values, aspirations, and character. The authenticity you channel through this guide will resonate powerfully, echoing a narrative that's both genuine and compelling.

A Symphony of Impact

Think of your branding journey as a symphony—an orchestration of elements that harmonize to create a resonating melody. The "Blue Book of Branding" serves as your conductor's baton, guiding each note, each design choice, and each visual element to compose a symphony of impact. It's through this symphony that you'll transcend the boundaries of communication, speaking directly to the hearts of parents, students, and the community.

A Call to Action and Transformation

In your pursuit of educational excellence, the "Blue

Book of Branding" isn't just a tool—it's a call to action and transformation. It invites you to step into the realm of creative empowerment, where concepts morph into reality, and aspirations take shape in visual form. As you open its pages, remember that every insight, every guideline, and every recommendation is an opportunity—an opportunity to create, to connect, and to transform your institution's narrative.

By embracing the wisdom woven into the fabric of the "Blue Book of Branding," you're not only embracing a guide; you're embracing the key to unlocking your institution's visual identity potential. It's your ticket to cultivating a branding resonance that lingers, forging connections that transcend the ordinary, and crafting an identity that's not just seen, but felt—an identity that leaves an indelible mark on hearts, minds, and the very essence of your educational institution.

Charting a Course for Brilliance

As we chart the course through this chapter, envision the "Blue Book of Branding" as your ally, accompanying you on a transformative odyssey. It's more than just a tool; it's a testament to your commitment to crafting a visual identity that captures the heart and soul of your institution. Whether you're a design enthusiast or a branding novice, this blueprint is designed to empower you to translate concepts into tangible masterpieces.

By offering the "Blue Book of Branding" as a complementary resource, we're extending a hand of partnership on your journey to brand brilliance. It's your secret weapon, ensuring your branding efforts are not just aligned but also amplified, driving your narrative to echo loud and clear across the educational landscape.

In this chapter, we've not only introduced the "Blue Book of Branding" but also ignited the spark for you to unlock its potential. As you venture further into the realms of educational branding, remember that this treasure trove of guidance isn't just a supplement—it's an opportunity to infuse precision and consistency into your branding, ensuring your institution's legacy shines brilliantly in every pixel, print, and interaction.

Let's step in ...

STEP 1: DEFINING YOUR VISUAL PALETTE

The Art And Science Of Color Storytelling

In the intricate realm of educational branding, colors are not merely shades; they are vibrant threads that weave the tapestry of your school's identity. As you embark on the journey of crafting a cohesive brand identity, the first stroke of your artistic brush introduces you to the captivating world of your visual palette—a world where each color is a storyteller, conveying emotions, values, and aspirations.

Color Philosophy: The Emotive Language of Hues

Colors possess a language all their own—a language that transcends words and resonates deep within the human psyche. Just as words carry meaning, colors communicate feelings, associations, and ideals. The "Blue Book of Branding" introduces you to the philosophy of colors—an art that involves choosing hues aligned with your institution's narrative. Each color carries its own voice: blue whispers trust and stability, green echoes growth and harmony, while red resonates with energy and passion. By embracing this philosophy, you empower colors to become eloquent messengers narrating your school's unique story.

Colors and the Brain: The Psychology of Perception

Behind every color lies a fascinating journey through the corridors of the brain. Colors have the power to evoke emotions, sway decisions, and shape perceptions. Understanding the psychology of colors grants you the ability to create an identity that resonates profoundly. The "Blue Book" delves into this psychology, unveiling how specific colors trigger distinct responses. The right color choice is more than visually appealing; it's strategically designed to align with your institution's values and evoke desired emotions.

Harmonizing with Your Audience: Colors that Resonate

Imagine your visual palette as a symphony—a symphony that harmonizes with the hearts and minds of your audience. By defining primary and secondary colors that mirror your school's essence, you're composing a visual melody that resonates deeply. The "Blue Book of Branding" offers guidance in selecting colors that not only capture attention but also forge a lasting connection. Every interaction with your branding materials becomes a melodious note in the symphony of your narrative.

Primary and Secondary Colors: Choosing Your Harmonious Palette

Primary Colors:

Sapphire Blue: Symbolizing trust, stability, and wisdom, sapphire blue is a timeless choice for educational institutions. It exudes a sense of reliability and responsibility, aligning perfectly with the educational journey you offer.

Emerald Green: Reflecting growth, harmony, and renewal, emerald green embodies the flourishing of knowledge and personal development within your school's nurturing environment.

Crimson Red: Evoking energy, passion, and vibrancy, crimson red resonates with the enthusiasm and vitality of both students and educators in their pursuit of excellence.

Secondary Colors:

Golden Yellow: Representing optimism, enlightenment, and wisdom, golden yellow complements your school's commitment to enlightening young minds and guiding them toward a brighter future.

Amethyst Purple: Symbolizing creativity, introspection, and inspiration, amethyst purple aligns with the intellectual exploration and imaginative growth that your institution fosters.

Harbor Gray: Conveying balance, professionalism, and neutrality, harbor gray provides a backdrop of stability that showcases your commitment to a structured yet innovative educational approach.

As you embark on the journey of defining your visual palette, consider these colors and their significance as a starting point. The "Blue Book of Branding" will offer deeper insights and practical guidance to ensure your selected colors resonate harmoniously with your school's spirit and values.

The Power of Consistency: Crafting Visual Cohesion

In a world of visual noise, consistency becomes a beacon of recognition. Your carefully defined visual palette becomes the glue that binds your branding elements into a harmonious narrative. By adhering to this palette, every flyer, every social media post, and every website banner becomes an eloquent expression of your school's identity, creating a visual symphony that echoes your ethos. This cohesion isn't just visually pleasing; it's strategically designed to evoke emotions and create an enduring connection with your audience —a connection woven through the language of colors.

STEP 2: CRAFTING THE EMBLEM OF IDENTITY

Forging The Symbol Of Your Soul

In the intricate tapestry of educational branding, your logo is not just a symbol—it's a living emblem of your institution's essence. It serves as the visual embodiment of your values, aspirations, and personality. As you venture into the art of creating a logo that truly breathes your identity, this chapter serves as your guiding light—a profound journey through the heart and soul of your school's visual representation.

Beyond Visuals: The Profound Essence of a Logo

A logo transcends its graphic form; it's a portal through which your institution's ethos flows effortlessly. Much like human faces tell tales of uniqueness, logos are the personification of your educational narrative. Under the guidance of the "Blue Book of Branding," you'll come to realize that a logo is more than just a design—it's a profound narrative condensed into visual form. It's your school's saga communicated through lines, curves, and hues.

A Glimpse into Your Identity: The Emblem's Significance

Your logo isn't merely an emblem; it's the mirror

reflecting your institution's identity to the world. With the "Blue Book" as your guiding star, you'll grasp that a logo is far more than ink on paper—it's a glimpse into the very heart of your educational journey. It carries the weight of your values and the wings of your aspirations, ready to take flight in the minds of your audience.

The Birth of an Icon: Crafting Your Visual Signature

In this step, you breathe life into your brand's visual signature—the logo. It's not just a design; it's an artistic manifestation of your institution's soul. With the "Blue Book of Branding" as your artistic mentor, you'll delve into the intricate process of crafting an emblem that resonates with your essence. This chapter unveils the secrets of transforming ideas into lines, curves, and shapes—a symphony that tells your story even before words are spoken.

A Symphony in Simplicity: The Art of Logo Design

Just as a melody can convey emotions without words, your logo encapsulates volumes within its simplicity. With the "Blue Book" as your creative companion, you'll explore the art of simplicity—an art that distills complexity into a single visual language. Every curve and stroke becomes a note in the symphony of your logo. Through simplicity, you'll uncover the power of resonance—a power that enables your logo to echo your institution's values across dimensions.

Craftsmanship and Creativity: The Journey of Identity

Creation

As you traverse this chapter, remember that crafting a logo is more than a design exercise—it's a journey that fuses craftsmanship and creativity. The "Blue Book of Branding" is your seasoned guide on this expedition, offering insights, tips, and techniques that transform your ideas into a visual masterpiece. With each stroke of your creative endeavor, you're forging an emblem that's more than a mere logo—it's an identity, a symbol, and a mirror reflecting your school's soul.

When considering logos for residential schools, it's important to create a design that captures the essence and values of the institution. Here are some logo concepts to consider, along with their reasoning:

Crest or Emblem Logo: A crest or emblem logo often incorporates symbols, shields, and intricate details. This type of logo can reflect the rich history and tradition of the school, emphasizing its academic excellence and strong heritage.

Book and Tree Symbolism: Incorporating an open book and a tree can symbolize growth, knowledge, and nurturing. It reflects the school's commitment to education while highlighting its focus on holistic development and a nurturing environment.

Building Silhouette: Using an iconic building silhouette of the school's main structure or a notable architectural element can create a strong visual association with the institution. This logo signifies a place of learning and community.

Student and Mentor: A logo that features a student and a mentor figure can showcase the school's dedication to personalized guidance and mentorship. This emphasizes the role of teachers in shaping students' lives.

Global Connection: If the school has an international focus, consider using elements that symbolize global connections, like a globe, compass, or interconnected lines. This logo represents the school's global outlook and commitment to cross-cultural learning.

Lighthouse: A lighthouse symbolizes guidance, safety, and leading the way. It can reflect the school's role in guiding students towards a brighter future and helping them navigate through their educational journey.

Infinite Loop: An infinity symbol can represent continuous learning, growth, and limitless possibilities. It showcases the school's commitment to providing lifelong education and fostering a growth mindset.

Mascot Logo: Creating a friendly and relatable mascot can personify the school's spirit and values. It can make the institution more approachable and resonate well with younger students.

Pathway and Gate: A logo featuring a pathway leading towards a gate can symbolize a journey towards knowledge and success. It emphasizes the school as a gateway to a better future through education.

Sunrise: Incorporating a sunrise can represent new beginnings, inspiration, and enlightenment. This logo signifies the school's role in shaping young minds and fostering a sense of optimism.

Remember, the logo should be simple, scalable, and versatile to work well across various applications, from stationery to digital platforms. Whichever concept you choose, it's important that the logo aligns seamlessly with the school's values, mission, and overall brand narrative..

STEP 3: TYPOGRAPHY THAT SPEAKS

The Dance Of Letters And Meaning

In the realm of educational branding, typography is not just a matter of selecting fonts—it's an art of conveying the very essence and character of your brand. This chapter unveils the delicate dance of letters and meaning, guiding you through the profound realm of typography. Here, we delve into the intricacies of font selection and unveil the power of typefaces to amplify your school's voice.

A Language Beyond Words: Typography's Voice

Typography is more than words on a page; it's a language that resonates with the reader's subconscious. Just as spoken words carry tone and emotion, typefaces carry a unique personality. The "Blue Book of Branding" leads you into the heart of this language, helping you understand how different fonts evoke various emotions. Each typeface is a brushstroke on the canvas of your school's narrative, painting a distinct mood and atmosphere.

The Personality of Fonts: Your Brand's Verbal Identity

Fonts possess personalities—they can be serious, playful, elegant, or modern. The choice of typeface isn't arbitrary; it's a deliberate reflection of your school's character. In the "Blue Book," you'll uncover the different personalities fonts can assume. Serif fonts exude tradition and respect, while sans-serif fonts signify modernity and simplicity. Script fonts evoke elegance, and display fonts showcase creativity. By understanding these personalities, you empower your written communication to resonate authentically.

Guiding the Reader: Typography's Navigation

Typography isn't just about aesthetics; it's about guiding the reader's experience. The "Blue Book" illuminates the art of hierarchy and readability. It helps you understand font sizes, spacing, and alignment —a symphony that orchestrates a seamless reading journey. Your chosen fonts, when paired thoughtfully, lead the reader's eye, emphasizing important information and enhancing the overall understanding of your content.

Crafting Consistency: The Typeface Symphony

Consistency is the heartbeat of branding, and typography is no exception. The "Blue Book of Branding" provides a roadmap to create a harmonious typeface symphony. By adhering to a specific font family for headings, subheadings, and body text, you ensure that your written communication sings with uniformity. This symphony of typefaces contributes to your brand's recognizability, making your content instantly identifiable.

Preferred Typeface Palette: Crafting Your School's Verbal

Identity

Serif Typeface (Traditional Elegance): Times New Roman, Georgia, Baskerville. A serif font lends an air of tradition and respect, making it suitable for formal communications and conveying a sense of established wisdom.

Sans-Serif Typeface (Modern Simplicity): Arial, Helvetica, Calibri. Sans-serif fonts exude modernity and simplicity, making them ideal for conveying a contemporary and approachable image.

Script Typeface (Elegant Sophistication): Cursive fonts like Pacifico, Great Vibes, and Allura. Script fonts convey elegance and sophistication, making them perfect for special announcements and creative expressions.

Display Typeface (Bold Creativity): Impact, Playfair Display, Lobster. Display fonts are bold and eye-catching, perfect for headlines and creative elements that demand attention.

As you navigate the waters of typography, remember that each font choice is a brushstroke in the masterpiece of your brand's communication. By adhering to the principles outlined in the "Blue Book," you're creating a visual and verbal symphony that resonates harmoniously with your school's spirit and values.

STEP 4: IMAGERY THAT RESONATES

The Visual Symphony Of Brand Identity

In the intricate symphony of educational branding, imagery is not just a decorative flourish—it's a profound language that resonates with the hearts and minds of your audience. This chapter illuminates the art of selecting and crafting images that amplify your institution's narrative. As you navigate the world of imagery, you'll realize that each visual element contributes harmoniously to the grand symphony of your brand's identity.

The Power of Visuals: An Unspoken Language

Images possess an innate ability to transcend words and communicate directly with emotions. Just as words narrate, and typography speaks, imagery evokes visceral feelings. The "Blue Book of Branding" introduces you to this unspoken language—a language that can convey stories, evoke sentiments, and communicate values with a single glance.

Choosing the Right Imagery: Echoing Your Identity

Each image should be more than a mere illustration—it should mirror the very essence of your brand. The "Blue Book" acts as your visual guide, aiding you in selecting imagery that seamlessly aligns with your school's values and narrative. Vibrant images radiating energy and growth, serene scenes reflecting tranquility and reflection, and dynamic visuals echoing innovation— each image becomes a vital note in your brand's visual melody.

The Art of Visual Techniques: Crafting Emotion through Imagery

Imagery is more than just a snapshot; it's a canvas for emotion and storytelling. The "Blue Book of Branding" introduces you to various visual techniques, such as vibrant color palettes, high key and low key lighting, duotone effects, and more. Each technique sets a unique tone and atmosphere, enabling you to narrate stories that resonate deeply. In a way, these visual elements act as punctuation marks in the story you're telling.

Crafting Custom Visuals: Unveiling Your Uniqueness

While selecting images is essential, crafting custom visuals elevates your brand's distinctiveness. The "Blue Book" unwraps the art of creating bespoke illustrations and graphics that are exclusively yours. From infographics that simplify complex ideas to custom illustrations that encapsulate your values, these visuals are brushstrokes of creativity that enrich your narrative.

Recommended Visual Palette for Schools:

Vibrant and Energetic: Images reflecting dynamic classroom interactions, sports activities, and extracurricular events. These images project vitality, energy, and enthusiasm, aligning with a school's commitment to holistic development.

Serene and Reflective: Visuals capturing serene campuses, peaceful study environments, and moments of introspection. These images evoke a sense of tranquility and mindfulness, resonating with an institution's emphasis on well-rounded growth.

Innovative and Cutting-Edge: Imagery showcasing technology integration, scientific experiments, and modern teaching methods. These visuals project innovation and progress, mirroring a school's dedication to staying at the forefront of education.

By adhering to the guidelines outlined in the "Blue Book of Branding," you ensure that every visual element harmonizes with your brand's narrative. The selection and creation of imagery become an artful endeavor that adds depth, authenticity, and resonance to your school's identity.

STEP 5: CONSISTENCY AND EXECUTION

The Backbone Of Lasting Impressions

In the grand tapestry of educational branding, consistency forms the unbreakable thread that weaves your narrative together. This chapter serves as the final crescendo—a reminder of the vital role that adhering to the guidelines set forth in the Blue Book plays in creating an indelible mark. From brochures to social media posts, from campus banners to digital newsletters, it's the execution of your branding assets that forges recognition and nurtures trust among your cherished audience.

Crafting a Harmonious Brand Symphony: Consistency at its Core

Imagine a symphony where each instrument plays a different tune—it would create chaos instead of melody. Similarly, branding thrives on consistency. The "Blue Book of Branding" instills in you the significance of executing your brand guidelines with unwavering commitment. Every element, whether it's the font choice, the color palette, or the imagery style, contributes to a harmonious symphony that resonates with authenticity.

Recognition Through Repetition: The Power of Consistency

Consistency isn't just about conformity; it's about creating a visual signature that becomes etched in memory. Repetition reinforces your brand's presence, making it familiar to your audience. The "Blue Book" unveils the potency of consistency—whether a parent stumbles upon your website, browses through a brochure, or scrolls through social media, the seamless execution of branding assets communicates your identity without uttering a word.

The Trust Factor: Consistency Breeds Credibility

Trust is the cornerstone of any enduring relationship, and branding is no exception. Consistency nurtures trust by showcasing your commitment to quality and authenticity. When every touchpoint aligns seamlessly with your brand's personality, it communicates reliability. The "Blue Book of Branding" accentuates the importance of this trust-building journey—consistency is the path that bridges perception and reality.

Holistic Campus Alignment: Every Corner, Every Expression

Branding extends beyond digital platforms; it encompasses every corner of your campus. From banners fluttering in the breeze to classroom walls adorned with visual motifs, every physical expression adheres to your brand's visual language. The "Blue Book" serves as your compass, guiding you in translating your brand's essence into tangible experiences that envelop your students, parents, and staff in a unified narrative.

Guided by the Blue Book: A Pledge to Consistency

As you stand at the threshold of executing your branding assets, remember that each design element, each word, and each visual representation holds the potential to reinforce your brand's identity. The "Blue Book of Branding" isn't merely a manual—it's a pledge to uphold the promises you've made through your brand narrative. By adhering to its guidelines, you create a symphony of consistency that echoes in the minds and hearts of your audience.

Elevating Trust and Connection: Through Consistency

Consistency isn't a rigid conformity; it's a dynamic practice that elevates trust and fosters a deeper connection. When you execute your branding assets consistently, you communicate reliability and authenticity. Every brochure, every digital post, every event banner is a brushstroke in your brand's canvas. As you navigate this final chapter, remember that the Blue Book's guidance is your guiding star, ensuring that your brand narrative resonates harmoniously, building bridges of recognition, trust, and lasting connection.

Empower Your Brand: Unleash the Power of Consistency

Imagine a world where every piece of your school's visual communication resonates with authenticity and purpose. A world where your branding materials don't just look good, but embody the very essence of your institution's identity. This world isn't a distant dream

—it's your reality, waiting to be unlocked through the transformative power of the Blue Book of Branding. This chapter is a call to action—a call to harness the steps, strategies, and insights within the Blue Book to propel your branding efforts to new heights.

A Blueprint for Harmonious Identity: Empowering Designers and Creators

The Blue Book of Branding isn't a mere guide; it's a blueprint for crafting a harmonious symphony of visual identity. By immersing yourself in its insights, you empower your designers and creators with the knowledge and tools needed to craft materials that go beyond aesthetics. Every design element, from typography to imagery, becomes a vessel to convey your school's vision and mission. With a unified visual identity, you're ensuring that every visual touchpoint, whether digital or physical, echoes the values your institution stands for.

The Magic of Consistency: Your Brand's Most Loyal Ally

Consistency isn't a mere concept—it's the secret ingredient that transforms your branding efforts from ordinary to extraordinary. With the Blue Book as your guide, you'll understand the magic that consistency weaves into your visual identity. Your brand will resonate harmoniously across diverse platforms and touchpoints, creating an unbroken thread that connects with your audience wherever they encounter it.

A Visual Identity that Amplifies Purpose: Echoing Vision and Mission

In your hands lies the power to shape a visual identity that resonates with the strength of your school's vision and mission. The Blue Book equips you to imbue every design, every color palette, and every image with the essence of your institution's purpose. Armed with this guidance, your brand transforms into a force— an identity that not only communicates but leaves an indelible mark on everyone it touches. It's about more than aesthetics; it's about infusing every design element with intention and purpose.

Seize the Opportunity: Your Brand's Transformation Awaits

The power to transform your brand lies within your reach, within the pages of the Blue Book of Branding. This chapter is a call to seize the opportunity—to dive into the strategies, embrace the wisdom, and apply the insights that will elevate your branding efforts to unprecedented heights. By embracing the Blue Book's guidance, you're not just crafting materials; you're crafting a legacy—a legacy of authenticity, recognition, and lasting impact.

Take Action Now: Unlock Your Brand's Potential

As you embark on this transformative journey, remember that the Blue Book isn't a passive resource —it's an active tool that propels your brand forward. Your designers will find direction, your creators will find inspiration, and your marketing teams will find a roadmap to success. Every step you take based on the Blue Book's insights is a step towards unlocking your brand's full potential, creating a visual identity that resonates, captivates, and endures. The power to transform your brand is in your hands—take action now and embrace the future you're destined to create.